FAITH AND HEALING

A Year of Gratitude, Happiness, Wellness, and Spiritual Awareness

INTRODUCTION

WELCOME

Welcome to "Faith and Healing: A Year of Gratitude, Happiness, Wellness, and Spiritual Awareness." This journal is more than just pages to fill; it's a companion on your journey toward a healthier, more fulfilled version of yourself. As you turn the pages, you'll find a guided exploration of gratitude, happiness, Wellness, and spiritual awareness.

NAVIGATING YOUR PERSONAL JOURNEY

The first chapters of this journal serve as a compass, providing definitions and explanations to guide your journaling journey. But remember, this is YOUR journal. The real magic happens when you engage with the content, reflect on the prompts, and pour your thoughts onto the pages. There's no rigid structure, no right or wrong way — just your way.

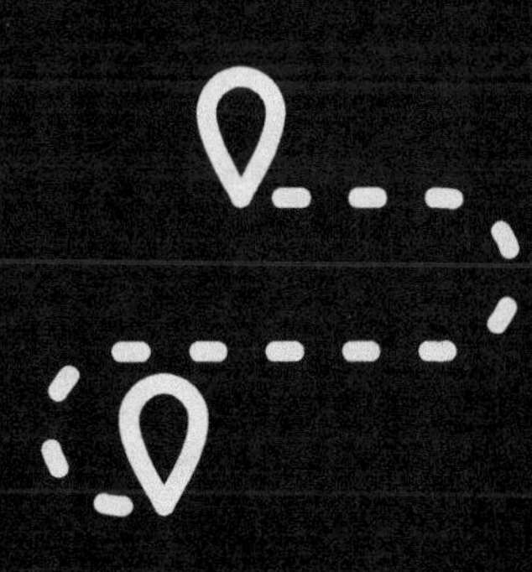

YOUR UNIQUE PATH TO WELLNESS

As you embark on this journey, embrace the understanding that wellness is a holistic concept. It is not just physical health but also emotional resilience, financial stability, and spiritual awareness. The journal is a tool to help you navigate and nurture each facet of your well-being.

INTRODUCTION

THE POWER OF JOURNALING

Journaling is your ally in this expedition. It's a space for introspection, a canvas for your thoughts, feelings, and aspirations. The key is not perfection but persistence. Allow your journal to be a witness to your growth, a confidant in your challenges, and a celebration of your victories. The journal is designed to allow you to journal daily or weekly depending on your preferences and schedule.

NO JUDGMENT, ONLY EXPLORATION

In the realm of personal development, there is no judgment, only exploration. This journal is a haven for your reflections, a mirror to your authentic self. Each day is an opportunity to discover something new about yourself and to foster gratitude, happiness, and a sense of connectedness.

YOUR COMMITMENT TO SELF-DISCOVERY

Remember, the essence of this journal lies in your commitment to self-discovery. It's not about completing every page but about engaging with the process. So, dive in, explore, and allow this journal to be a catalyst for positive change in your life.

May this year-long journey be transformative and may the pages of this journal reflect the beautiful evolution of your inner self. Happy journaling!

Pledge of Commitment to Self-Discovery:

Embarking on a journey of self-discovery is a powerful and transformative endeavor. It is a commitment to understanding oneself, embracing growth, and fostering a positive relationship with the person you are becoming. As we embark on this journey together, I invite you to solidify your dedication through the Pledge of Commitment to Self-Discovery.

This pledge is a personal contract, a promise you make to yourself. It's a reminder that, as you navigate the complexities of life, you will extend grace, celebrate victories, and confront challenges with resilience and compassion. Through this commitment, you lay the foundation for a journey marked by self-love, authenticity, and continual growth.

Please take a moment to reflect on each statement in the pledge and personalize it with your own intentions. As you affirm your commitment, recognize the power that lies within you to shape your own narrative and cultivate a fulfilling and meaningful life.

This is your pledge, your promise to yourself. May it guide you on this transformative journey of self-discovery.

Pledge of Commitment to Self-Discovery:

I, ____,

hereby commit to the journey of self-discovery with an unwavering pledge to extend grace to myself. In this pursuit, I embrace the following principles:

1. I will extend myself grace:
   - In moments of challenge and growth, I will offer myself the same kindness and understanding that I readily extend to others.
   - I will acknowledge that perfection is an unrealistic standard, and I am allowed to be a work in progress.

2. I will honor my victories no matter how small:
   - I will celebrate every achievement, recognizing that progress, no matter how incremental, is a cause for celebration.
   - Each step forward is a testament to my strength, resilience, and commitment to self-improvement.

3. I will celebrate and focus on the good things in my life:
   - I will cultivate an attitude of gratitude, acknowledging the positive aspects of my life.
   - I will intentionally shift my focus toward joy, acknowledging the blessings and moments of happiness.

4. I will acknowledge and address the unpleasant ones:
- I will face challenges with courage, understanding that they are growth opportunities.
- I will address areas of discomfort with honesty and a commitment to positive change.

5. I will approach self-discovery with an open heart:
- I will be open to learning more about myself, acknowledging both strengths and areas for improvement.
- I will embrace self-reflection as a tool for personal growth and development.

6. I will foster a positive and compassionate mindset:
- I will speak to myself with kindness, encouraging words, and the understanding that I am deserving of love and compassion.
- I will nurture a positive inner dialogue that supports my well-being and fosters self-love.

7. I will prioritize self-care:
- I will recognize the importance of my mental, emotional, and physical well-being.
- I will carve out time for activities that bring me joy, relaxation, and rejuvenation.

8. I will remain committed to the journey of self-discovery:
- I understand that self-discovery is an ongoing process, and I commit to embracing every twist and turn in the path.
- I will approach challenges as opportunities to learn more about myself and to evolve into the best version of myself.

With this pledge, I embark on a journey of self-discovery, armed with compassion, celebration, and an unwavering commitment to becoming the most authentic and fulfilled version of myself.

A year of Nurturing the Seeds of Gratitude and Self-Appreciation

As the clock resets and the calendar turns, we find ourselves standing at the threshold of a new year, a canvas waiting to be painted with the hues of experiences, growth, and gratitude.

Words are Important

Before we start our year and get caught up in the various ups and downs we will experience on our journey, let's ground ourselves in the understanding of gratitude. Gratitude is defined as the quality of being thankful; and readiness to show appreciation for and to return kindness. This goes beyond a perfunctory "thank you," gratitude is an attitude — a lens through which we view the world. It's a quality that transforms routine gestures of appreciation into a way of being, enriching our interactions and shaping our outlook.

Understanding the Year

As we set sail into the unknown waters of the next 365 days, let's anchor ourselves in the understanding of a year. It's not merely a unit of time but a vessel carrying the cargo of our experiences, trials, and triumphs. A year encapsulates the seasons of life, marked by transitions, lessons, and the ever-present opportunity for growth.

Gratitude Toward Ourselves

In the ebb and flow of life, it's easy to overlook an essential practice — expressing gratitude towards oneself. The endeavors, both seen and unseen, have contributed to the evolution of who we are today. As we embark on this year-long journey, let us carve out intentional moments to acknowledge our efforts, the silent battles fought, and the personal victories achieved.

Gratitude towards oneself is not an act of vanity but a foundation for self-love and resilience. It's a recognition of the strength that resides within, enabling us to face the challenges that each new year inevitably brings.

The Rare Art of Acknowledgment

In a world characterized by speed and perpetual motion, the genuine acknowledgment of others can be a rare and precious gift. How often do we extend gratitude to those who have shared our journey, offering support, understanding, or a simple act of kindness? Gratitude is not just a courtesy; it's a transformative force that deepens connections and fosters a sense of community.

Commencing the Journey with Gratitude

So, as we set sail into this new year, let gratitude be our North Star. This exploration is not just a daily practice; it's a commitment to weaving gratitude into the very fabric of our lives. By understanding and embracing gratitude, we not only enhance our personal well-being but also contribute to a collective consciousness where appreciation and kindness are the cornerstones.

In the next 52 weeks, may each sunrise bring a new opportunity to express gratitude, to ourselves and to those who walk beside us. Let this be a year of growth, healing, and spiritual awareness, guided by the compass of gratitude that points us towards a richer, more fulfilling journey.

Gratitude Journaling

A gratitude journal is more than a collection of words on paper; it is a mirror reflecting the richness of our lives. Its pages invite us to pause, reflect, and express gratitude for the moments that might otherwise slip through the cracks of our busy lives. By consciously acknowledging and recording the things we are thankful for, we create a tangible testament to the positive aspects of our existence.

This year, the challenge is to time out, whether in the stillness of the morning or the quietude of the evening, to identify at least one thing you are grateful for. It could be a moment, a person, a realization, or a simple pleasure.

You should also extend the same lens of appreciation towards yourself. In the rush of daily life, we often forget to acknowledge our own efforts, strengths, and unique qualities. Each day, make it a practice to identify at least one thing you appreciate about yourself. It could be a small achievement, a quality you displayed, or an act of kindness towards yourself. This daily act of self-appreciation becomes a ripple that transforms the way you perceive yourself. By consciously recognizing and expressing gratitude, you invite positivity into your day.

Embracing the Gift of Now: A Year of Living in the Moment and Being Happy

In the perpetual pursuit of happiness, we often find ourselves caught in the web of the future, planning and scheming, and in the regrets of the past, replaying moments and analyzing decisions. The irony lies in the fact that, during this quest, we seldom allow ourselves the simple joy of being happy in the present moment. It took a poignant remark during an argument to awaken the realization that we might not truly experience ourselves — a revelation that unveils the multifaceted nature of happiness.

Words Matter: Defining Happiness

Before we embark on this journey, let's delve into the definition of happiness. It is more than a fleeting emotion or a destination to be reached. Happiness, as defined, is the state of being happy — a sense of pleasure, contentment, and confidence. It is fortunate, convenient, and, most importantly, within our grasp in the present moment.

The Profound Revelation

"You don't experience you." These words, uttered to me by my partner in the heat of an argument, echo with profound truth. Beyond the immediate context, they unravel two layers of significance. The first layer exposes our blind spot — the inability to witness and understand how we affect the people around us. The second layer, perhaps more crucial, speaks to the paradox of our pursuit of happiness — we are so consumed by the pursuit that we forget to savor the happiness that exists in our current experiences.

The Challenge of Living in the Moment

As we venture into this year of exploration, the challenge is clear: to live in the moment, to grant ourselves permission to truly experience life, and, above all, to be happy. Happiness, often elusive, is not a distant destination but a state of being. It is not found in the relentless chase for the next achievement or milestone; rather, it resides in the small, often overlooked, moments of joy that pepper our everyday existence.

The Now Matters

Living in the moment is not a call to abandon dreams or cease planning for the future. It is an invitation to be present, to savor the richness of the current chapter, and to acknowledge the happiness that exists in the now. It's about recognizing the beauty in the mundane, finding joy in the ordinary, and appreciating the precious gift of each moment.

Giving Ourselves Permission

The challenge lies not in the complexity of the task but in granting ourselves permission to be happy. It involves letting go of the guilt associated with taking a break from the relentless pursuit of goals and success. It entails embracing the belief that happiness is not an external achievement but an internal state of mind that can be cultivated and nurtured.

Cultivating Happiness Daily

As we navigate the days ahead, let happiness be a daily practice. In your journaling, make space not only for the things you are thankful for but also for the moments that brought you joy. Challenge yourself to find happiness in unexpected places, in the laughter of a friend, in the warmth of sunlight, or in the aroma of your favorite meal.

A Holistic Approach: A Year of Health, Wealth, and Well-being

As the calendar turns its pages, ushering in a new year, the familiar ritual of setting resolutions echoes across countless minds. Gym memberships, weight loss goals, financial ambitions, and promises to strengthen family bonds often fill our lists. Yet, more often than not, these resolutions fade into the background by February or March, forgotten or abandoned. In this chapter, we embark on a journey not just of resolutions but of a holistic commitment to health, wealth, and well-being — a pursuit that goes beyond fleeting promises.

Words Matter

The term "wellness" has permeated our language, often conjuring images of spa days and relaxation. Wellness is defined as the state of being in good health, especially as an actively pursued goal. However, at its core, wellness is about achieving and maintaining homeostasis — a stable equilibrium between interdependent elements. It extends beyond physical pampering to encompass the delicate balance of life and work, healthy interpersonal relationships, and realistic habits regarding diet and exercise.

The Essence of Homeostasis

Creating homeostasis in our lives involves consciously nurturing equilibrium in various aspects. It requires us to evaluate and redefine our relationships, set realistic boundaries, and cultivate habits that contribute to our overall well-being. This year, we commit to not only recognizing but actively pursuing the delicate balance that homeostasis entails.

The Holistic Definition of Wellness

Let's redefine wellness beyond its conventional bounds. Wellness is not confined to physical health; it is a dynamic state that encompasses emotional, financial, and spiritual well-being. As we explore the facets of wellness this year, our focus extends to the pursuit of good health actively, intentionally nurturing emotional resilience, fostering financial stability, and deepening our spiritual connection.

Beyond Physical Health

This year, health transcends the conventional understanding of diet and exercise. It incorporates mental well-being, emotional resilience, and the cultivation of healthy habits that contribute to a balanced and vibrant life. As we set health goals, let them be inclusive — addressing not only physical fitness but also mental clarity and emotional strength.

The Wealth of Holistic Prosperity

Wealth, too, takes on a broader definition. It is not just financial abundance but encompasses a richness of experiences, relationships, and personal growth. This year, our commitment to wealth extends beyond monetary goals to include the pursuit of enriching experiences, meaningful connections, and personal development.

Nurturing Emotional and Spiritual Well-being

Emotional well-being involves understanding and managing our emotions, fostering resilience, and cultivating positive relationships. Meanwhile, spiritual well-being encompasses a connection to something greater than ourselves — whether it be through faith, mindfulness, or a sense of purpose. This year, we actively pursue these dimensions of well-being, recognizing their impact on our overall health and happiness.

The Holistic Journey Begins

As we step into this chapter of health, wealth, and well-being, let our commitment be grounded not in fleeting resolutions but in a year-long journey of intentional living. Let the pursuit of balance, resilience, and abundance guide our decisions and actions. By the end of this year, may we find ourselves not only healthier and wealthier but also in a state of holistic well-being, enriched in every facet of our lives.

Awakening the Spirit Within: A Year of Spiritual Awareness

When the topic of spirituality arises, our minds often gravitate toward religious doctrines and prescribed ways of connecting with a higher power. For many, the notion of spirituality may be tinged with negative experiences associated with rigid religious practices that often confine and control. This year we are going to reframe our understanding of spirituality, recognizing it as an innate aspect of our being that extends beyond religious boundaries.

Words Matter

Spirituality is defined as the quality of being concerned with the human spirit or soul.Spirituality transcends the confines of material or physical realms. It is a connection to something beyond ourselves, a yearning for a deeper understanding of existence. While religion and spirituality are often intertwined, they are distinct. Religion involves acts of worship or service, while spirituality is rooted in, our personal belief and connectedness to a higher power.

The Shadows of Religion

For some, the word "spirituality" may evoke memories of religious affiliations that were not chosen but rather inherited. Many have been shaped by the faith practices of their families, practices that may have been wielded as tools of control rather than pathways to spiritual awakening. This year, let us liberate spirituality from the shadows of religion and explore it as a deeply personal and independent journey.

Embracing Individual Expression

This year, understanding the nuances between religion and spirituality becomes paramount. While religious practices may serve as expressions of our spirituality, they do not define it. Spirituality is a personal identification with a higher power, a connection that goes beyond the rituals of organized worship. It is a deeply individual journey, untethered by external norms.

The Call to Explore

Our focus in the coming months is on exploring our own spirituality and connectedness. It's an invitation to unravel the threads that tie us to the world around us. Spirituality, in its essence, is a personal experience — there is no right or wrong way, only your way. The goal is not conformity but a deep sense of connection and balance that nurtures the spiritual bond within.

Finding Your Connection

Take this year as an opportunity to discover how you connect to the world beyond the material. Whether through contemplative practices, nature, art, or introspection, the avenues are diverse. Spirituality is a canvas, and you are the artist — paint your connection in the colors that resonate with your soul.

Embracing Balance

The ultimate goal is to feel spiritually connected and balanced. Nurturing this connection involves introspection, exploration, and a willingness to be open to the vast possibilities that spiritual awareness can offer. As we delve into this chapter, let us do so with an open heart, embracing the uniqueness of our individual spiritual journeys.

No Right or Wrong

In the realm of spirituality, there is no template to follow, no right or wrong way. Each step you take is a brushstroke on the canvas of your own spiritual landscape. This year, let your exploration be guided by curiosity, authenticity, and the simple desire to understand the depths of your own spiritual being.

The Journey Begins Within

As we embark on this year of spiritual awareness, let the journey be an inward one. Explore, question, and connect with the profound spirit within. May this exploration lead to a deeper understanding of yourself and your place in existence.

Goal Setting for Holistic Well-being

As we embark on the journey it's essential to lay the groundwork for our transformation. This chapter is dedicated to the art of goal setting—a crucial step in crafting a healthier version of yourself. Goals act as guiding stars, illuminating the path toward holistic well-being. In setting these goals, we adhere to the SMART criteria: Specific, Measurable, Achievable, Realistic, and Time Bound.

The Power of Specificity

Specificity is the cornerstone of effective goal setting. Instead of vague aspirations, define your objectives with precision. Rather than saying "exercise more," specify "engage in 30 minutes of brisk walking every morning." The more detailed and concrete your goals, the clearer your path to success.

The Measure of Success

Measurability ensures that your progress is tangible. Establish metrics to track your journey. If your goal is to cultivate gratitude, specify measurable actions, like jotting down three things you're thankful for every day. This way, you can witness and celebrate your evolution.

Bridging the Gap to Achievability

While ambition is commendable, goals must be achievable. Set targets that stretch you but remain within the realm of feasibility. If your wellness goal involves dietary changes, start with realistic adjustments instead of radical shifts. Achievable goals build a foundation for lasting change.

The Reality Check of Realism

Goals must be grounded in realism. Consider your strengths, limitations, and the scope of change you can realistically embrace within a year. If your objective is spiritual awareness, set aside realistic time commitments for practices like meditation or mindfulness.

The Essence of Time Bound

A goal without a deadline is a mere intention. Time-bound goals provide a sense of urgency and structure. Define when you intend to achieve each goal. If your happiness goal involves cultivating a new hobby, set milestones for skill development within specific time frames.

Embracing Lifestyle Change

Our ultimate goal is holistic health, which entails a lifestyle change. Many of your goals will involve adopting new behaviors and ways of thinking. Recognize that this journey extends beyond the confines of a year; it's an ongoing process of growth and evolution.

Crafting Your Personal Wellness Blueprint

As you embark on this goal-setting journey, envision your goals as pillars supporting your holistic well-being. What do you want to achieve in gratitude, happiness, wellness, and spiritual awareness? Write them down, make them SMART, and let them serve as the foundation for your transformative journey.

Reflection and Refinement

Periodically revisit your goals, reflecting on your progress and refining them as needed. Allow your goals to be flexible, adapting to the changing landscape of your life. In this chapter, you're not just setting goals; you're shaping the architecture of your personal well-being.

May your goals be the stepping stones to a healthier, happier, and more fulfilled you. Let this chapter be the beginning of a transformative journey that unfolds with each passing day.

Sample Goals

Here are some examples of goals you may use, or you can create your own:

Gratitude:

1. **Goal: Cultivate a daily gratitude practice.**
   - Progress: Regularly noting down three things I'm grateful for each day.
   - Reflection: Still finding joy in acknowledging the positive aspects of my life.
   - Self-Acknowledgment: I've consistently made time for gratitude, which has positively impacted my mindset.

2. **Goal: Express gratitude to others.**
   - Progress: Shared appreciation with friends and family.
   - Reflection: It feels rewarding to strengthen relationships through gratitude.
   - Self-Acknowledgment: Successfully integrated expressing gratitude into my daily interactions.

Happiness:

1. **Goal: Engage in activities that bring joy.**
   - Progress: Prioritized activities I enjoy, such as reading and spending time in nature.
   - Reflection: These activities contribute to my overall happiness and well-being.
   - Self-Acknowledgment: I've succeeded in incorporating more joy into my daily life.

2. Goal: Practice mindfulness for increased happiness.

- Progress: Regularly practicing mindfulness exercises.
- Reflection: Mindfulness has improved my ability to stay present and find joy in small moments.
- Self-Acknowledgment: Making steady progress in cultivating a mindful mindset.

Spirituality:

1. Goal: Establish a spiritual routine (meditation, prayer, etc.).
   - Progress: Started a daily meditation practice.
   - Reflection: Feeling more centered and connected.
   - Self-Acknowledgment: Successfully initiated a spiritual routine, acknowledging the importance of this practice.

2. Goal: Attend spiritual gatherings or events.

- Progress: Participated in a local spiritual group.
- Reflection: Connecting with like-minded individuals is enriching.
- Self-Acknowledgment: Successfully integrated spiritual community involvement into my life.

Wellness:

1. **Goal: Prioritize mental well-being.**

- Progress: Engaged in regular journaling and self-reflection.
- Reflection: Journaling has been a helpful tool for mental clarity.
- Self-Acknowledgment: Consistently taking steps to prioritize my mental health.

My Goals this year are:

GRATITUDE:

____

____

____

____

HAPPINESS:

____

____

____

____

My Goals this year are:

WELLNESS

SPIRITUALITY

Journal for Holistic Well-being

As you navigate this year, journaling becomes your compass, guiding you through the intricate landscape of your well-being. In this chapter, we delve into the intricacies of daily journaling, a practice designed to illuminate your path to a healthier, more fulfilled version of yourself.

Gratitude: Cultivating Appreciation

Begin your journaling with a moment of gratitude. Reflect on the things you are thankful for, acknowledging the blessings in your life. This is not just about grand gestures; it's about the simple joys, the subtle victories, and the moments that warm your heart. Additionally, express appreciation for yourself — your strengths, your efforts, and the unique qualities that define you.

Happiness: Nurturing Personal Joy

Move on to the happiness section, where you chronicle the things, you allowed yourself to experience and do for your personal happiness. Did you engage in a hobby, connect with a friend, or savor a quiet moment of solitude? Capture the essence of what brought joy to your day, recognizing that happiness is both a pursuit and a state of being.

Wellness: Balancing Mind, Body, and Finances

Dedicate a section to wellness, acknowledging the multidimensional nature of your well-being. Reflect on the things you have done for your mental well-being — whether it's practicing mindfulness, engaging in a creative pursuit, or seeking moments of tranquility. Explore the actions you took for your physical well-being, be it exercise, nourishing meals, or restful sleep. Finally, consider the steps you have taken for your fiscal well-being, recognizing the importance of financial health in the holistic wellness journey.

Spiritual Awareness: Nourishing the Soul

The spiritual section of your journal is a sacred space to explore your connection to something greater than yourself. Document the things you have done to explore your spirituality — whether it is meditation, prayer, or moments of reflection. Chronicle the lessons you have learned about your spiritual self, recognizing the evolving nature of this exploration. Reflect on the times and ways when you feel most grounded spiritually, identifying the practices that anchor your soul.

A Ritual of Self-Reflection

Journaling is more than a record-keeping exercise; it is a ritual of self-reflection. It is a moment to pause, acknowledge, and celebrate the facets of your well-being. As you put pen to paper, let your journal be a mirror reflecting the intricate mosaic of your daily experiences, thoughts, and emotions.

Embracing Consistency

Consistency is the heartbeat of journaling. Set aside a dedicated time each week to engage in this practice. Whether it's in the morning, before bedtime, or during a quiet moment in your day, let journaling become a consistent companion on your journey to holistic well-being.

The Unfolding Journey

As you embark on this practice of journaling, let each entry be a stepping stone in the unfolding journey of self-discovery. Cherish the process, and let your journal be a testimony to the growth, resilience, and beauty inherent in your daily experiences.
May your journaling be a source of clarity, self-compassion, and empowerment. Let the pages be a testament to the rich and transformative journey toward a healthier, happier, and more spiritually aware you.

WELCOME TO JANUARY

Welcome to January, the inaugural month of the year, marking the commencement of the first quarter. As we embark on this new chapter, our focus for the month is guided by profound weekly thoughts, each holding a key to a richer and more meaningful life:

Week One: "Health is wealth; invest in yourself daily." January begins with a reminder that true wealth lies in our health. This week encourages us to make daily investments in ourselves—nurturing our physical and mental well-being. By prioritizing health, we lay the foundation for a vibrant and fulfilling life.

Week Two: "Happiness is a journey, not a destination; enjoy the ride." In the second week, we embrace the wisdom that happiness is not a distant destination but a continuous journey. Let's savor the moments, finding joy in the process, and appreciating the beauty of the ride. Happiness is woven into the fabric of our daily experiences.

Week Three: "Listen to the whispers of your soul; spiritual awareness is the compass of inner wisdom." Mid-January invites us to turn inward and heed the whispers of our souls. Spiritual awareness becomes the compass guiding us toward inner wisdom. This week encourages a deeper connection with our spiritual selves, fostering a profound understanding of our purpose and journey.

WELCOME TO JANUARY

Week Four: "Gratitude turns ordinary moments into extraordinary blessings." As we conclude January, the spotlight turns to gratitude. This week emphasizes the transformative power of gratitude, turning ordinary moments into extraordinary blessings. Let's cultivate a thankful heart, finding beauty in the simplicity of everyday life.

Join us in this January journey, where each week unfolds a new facet of health, happiness, spiritual awareness, and the magic of gratitude. Together, let's embark on this enriching exploration, laying the groundwork for a year filled with well-being, joy, wisdom, and appreciation.

January

Week 1 – Thought of the week, "Health is wealth; invest in yourself daily."
This week I will take the following steps on my journey:

GRATITUDE

____

____

____

____

HAPPINESS

____

____

____

____

WELLNESS

____

____

____

____

SPIRITUAL AWARENESS

____

____

____

____

Ðaily Journal

Daily Journal

Daily Journal

Daily Journal

Daily Journal

Daily Journal

January

Week 2 – Thought of the week, "Happiness is a journey, not a destination; enjoy the ride."

This week I will take the following steps on my journey:

GRATITUDE

____

____

____

____

HAPPINESS

____

____

____

____

WELLNESS

____

____

____

____

SPIRITUAL AWARENESS

____

____

____

____

Ðaily Journal

Ðaily Journal

Ðaily Journal

Daily Journal

Daily Journal

Daily Journal

Daily Journal

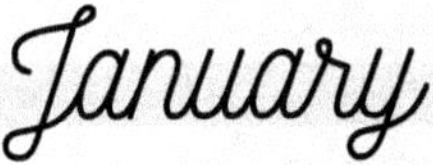 January

Week 3 – Thought of the week, "Listen to the whispers of your soul; spiritual awareness is the compass of inner wisdom."
This week I will take the following steps on my journey:

GRATITUDE

____

____

____

____

HAPPINESS

____

____

____

____

WELLNESS

____

____

____

____

SPIRITUAL AWARENESS

____

____

____

____

Daily Journal

Daily Journal

Daily Journal

Ðaily Journal

Đaily Journal

Daily Journal

Daily Journal

January

Week 4 – Thought of the week, "Gratitude turns ordinary moments into extraordinary blessings."
This week I will take the following steps on my journey:

GRATITUDE

____

____

____

____

HAPPINESS

____

____

____

____

WELLNESS

____

____

____

____

SPIRITUAL AWARENESS

____

____

____

____

Ðaily Journal

Daily Journal

Daily Journal

Daily Journal

Ðaily Journal

Đaily Journal

Daily Journal

MONTHLY SPENDING TRACKER

DATE: _______________

DATE	AMOUNT	DESCRIPTION	CASH	CARD
			☐	☐
			☐	☐
			☐	☐
			☐	☐
			☐	☐
			☐	☐
			☐	☐
			☐	☐
			☐	☐
			☐	☐
			☐	☐
			☐	☐
			☐	☐
			☐	☐

NOTES:

____

____

____

WELCOME TO FEBRUARY

Welcome to February, where our focus aligns with four enriching thoughts that pave the way for a month of well-being and positivity:

Welcome to February, a month dedicated to cultivating well-being and embracing positivity through our detailed weekly thoughts:

Week One: "In the garden of life, gratitude is the seed that blooms into joy." As we embark on this month, let's plant the seed of gratitude, nurturing it into moments of pure joy. Acknowledging and appreciating the beauty around us can transform our experience of life.

Week Two: "In the silence within, discover the universe of your spirit." Take a moment for introspection and delve into the quiet spaces within. In the stillness, explore the vast universe of your spirit, uncovering the depth and wisdom that reside in the core of your being.

Week Three: "Smile often; it's the simplest stitch to mend a tough day." A simple smile has the power to mend the toughest days. Let's spread positivity by embracing the simplicity of a smile, not only brightening our own days but also creating a ripple effect of joy around us.

WELCOME TO FEBRUARY

Week Four: "Fuel your body with kindness, and it will thank you with vitality." Nourish your body with acts of kindness. Whether through mindful nutrition or self-care, investing in your well-being will result in a vitality that echoes gratitude for the care you provide.

Join us on this journey throughout February as we plant seeds of gratitude, explore the vast universe within, spread joy with a simple smile, and prioritize the vitality of our bodies through acts of kindness. Each week let's embrace these principles and create a month filled with positivity and self-care.

February

Week 1 Thought of the week, "In the garden of life, gratitude is the seed that blooms into joy."

This week I will take the following steps on my journey:

GRATITUDE

____

____

____

____

HAPPINESS

____

____

____

____

WELLNESS

____

____

____

____

SPIRITUAL AWARENESS

____

____

____

____

Daily Journal

Daily Journal

Daily Journal

Daily Journal

Daily Journal

Ðaily Journal

Daily Journal

February

Week 2 Thought of the week, "In the silence within, discover the universe of your spirit."

This week I will take the following steps on my journey:

GRATITUDE

____

____

____

HAPPINESS

____

____

____

____

WELLNESS

____

____

____

____

SPIRITUAL AWARENESS

____

____

____

Đaily Journal

Đaily Journal

Daily Journal

Ðaily Journal

Daily Journal

Daily Journal

Daily Journal

February

Week 3 Thought of the week, "Smile often; it's the simplest stitch to mend a tough day."

This week I will take the following steps on my journey:

GRATITUDE

____

____

____

____

HAPPINESS

____

____

____

____

WELLNESS

____

____

____

____

SPIRITUAL AWARENESS

____

____

____

____

Ðaily Journal

Ðaily Journal

Daily Journal

Ðaily Journal

Ðaily Journal

Daily Journal

Daily Journal

February

Week 4 Thought of the week, "Fuel your body with kindness, and it will thank you with vitality."
This week I will take the following steps on my journey:

GRATITUDE

____

____

____

____

HAPPINESS

____

____

____

____

WELLNESS

____

____

____

____

SPIRITUAL AWARENESS

____

____

____

____

Ðaily Journal

Daily Journal

Daily Journal

Daily Journal

Ðaily Journal

Daily Journal

Ðaily Journal

MONTHLY SPENDING TRACKER

DATE: ______________

DATE	AMOUNT	DESCRIPTION	CASH	CARD
			☐	☐
			☐	☐
			☐	☐
			☐	☐
			☐	☐
			☐	☐
			☐	☐
			☐	☐
			☐	☐
			☐	☐
			☐	☐
			☐	☐
			☐	☐
			☐	☐

NOTES:

____

____

____

WELCOME TO MARCH

As we bid farewell to the first quarter of the year, March unfolds with a focus on rejuvenation, gratitude, purpose, and the transformative power of a grateful heart. Join us in exploring these profound thoughts that mark our journey through the end of the quarter:

Week One: "Move with purpose; exercise is a celebration of what your body can do." March begins with a call to move with intention, recognizing that exercise is not merely a routine but a celebration of the remarkable capabilities inherent in our bodies. Let's embark on this week with purposeful movements that honor and celebrate our physical well-being.

Week Two: "In the book of life, the happiest chapters are written with gratitude." As we turn the pages of life's book, let gratitude be the ink that writes our happiest chapters. This week invites us to acknowledge the abundance in our lives and embrace the joy that gratitude brings to every moment.

Week Three: "Awaken the spirit within; it's the key to unlocking a life of purpose." In the heart of March, let's focus on awakening our inner spirit. This thought encourages us to delve deep, unlocking the key to a life rich with purpose. Discovering and nurturing our inner spirit propels us toward a more meaningful existence.

WELCOME TO MARCH

Week Four: "A grateful heart is a magnet for miracles." As we conclude the month and the first quarter, cultivate a grateful heart. Recognize that gratitude acts as a powerful magnet, attracting miracles into our lives. March concludes with the reminder that a heart filled with gratitude opens the door to extraordinary possibilities.

Join us in this March journey, acknowledging the completion of the first quarter, as we move with purpose, write joyous chapters with gratitude, awaken our inner spirits, and become magnets for the miracles that await.

 March

Week 1 Thought of the week, "Move with purpose; exercise is a celebration of what your body can do."

This week I will take the following steps on my journey:

GRATITUDE

____

____

____

____

HAPPINESS

____

____

____

____

WELLNESS

____

____

____

____

SPIRITUAL AWARENESS

____

____

____

____

Daily Journal

Ðaily Journal

Daily Journal

Daily Journal

Daily Journal

Đaily Journal

Daily Journal

March

Week 2 Thought of the week, "In the book of life, the happiest chapters are written with gratitude."
This week I will take the following steps on my journey:

GRATITUDE

____
____
____
____

HAPPINESS

____
____
____
____

WELLNESS

____
____
____
____

SPIRITUAL AWARENESS

____
____
____
____

Daily Journal

Đaily Journal

Ðaily Journal

Daily Journal

Ðaily Journal

Ðaily Journal

Ðaily Journal

Week 3 Thought of the week, "Awaken the spirit within; it's the key to unlocking a life of purpose."
This week I will take the following steps on my journey:

GRATITUDE

____
____
____
____

HAPPINESS

____
____
____
____

WELLNESS

____
____
____
____

SPIRITUAL AWARENESS

____
____
____
____

Ðaily Journal

Daily Journal

Ðaily Journal

Daily Journal

Daily Journal

Daily Journal

Daily Journal

Week 4 Thought of the week, "A grateful heart is a magnet for miracles."
This week I will take the following steps on my journey:

GRATITUDE

____

____

____

____

HAPPINESS

____

____

____

____

WELLNESS

____

____

____

____

SPIRITUAL AWARENESS

____

____

____

____

Daily Journal

Daily Journal

Ðaily Journal

Daily Journal

Ðaily Journal

Daily Journal

Daily Journal

SPENDING TRACKER

DATE: ___________________

DATE	AMOUNT	DESCRIPTION	CASH	CARD
			☐	☐
			☐	☐
			☐	☐
			☐	☐
			☐	☐
			☐	☐
			☐	☐
			☐	☐
			☐	☐
			☐	☐
			☐	☐
			☐	☐
			☐	☐
			☐	☐

NOTES:

____

____

____

First Quarter Check-In on Goals

As we navigate the journey of personal growth and well-being, it's crucial to periodically pause and assess our progress. The first quarter check-in serves as a valuable opportunity to reflect on the goals set in the realms of Gratitude, Happiness, Spirituality, and Wellness. This intentional review is not about self-judgment but rather a compassionate examination of the path we've walked and the strides we've made.

In this check-in, we will engage in a thoughtful exploration of each dimension—Gratitude, Happiness, Spirituality, and Wellness. We'll celebrate achievements, acknowledge challenges, and, most importantly, extend grace to ourselves. The commitment to not berate ourselves for unmet goals is a vital aspect of this process. Instead, we'll focus on the progress achieved and consider adjustments that align with our evolving understanding of personal well-being.

As we embark on this check-in, let us approach it with an open heart and a spirit of self-compassion. Each goal is a step toward a more fulfilling life, and this review is a roadmap for continued growth and resilience. So, let's delve into the reflections on Gratitude, Happiness, Spirituality, and Wellness, embracing the opportunity for self-discovery and renewal.

My Goals

GRATITUDE

____

____

____

____

HAPPINESS

____

____

____

____

WELLNESS

____

____

____

____

SPIRITUAL AWARENESS

____

____

____

QUARTERLY SPENDING TRACKER

DUE DATE	BILL NAME	AMOUNT	PAID

INCOME	EXPENSES	PROFIT

General Reflection:

- Recognize the interconnectedness of gratitude, happiness, spirituality, and wellness.
- Note any challenges faced and identify strategies for overcoming them.
- Celebrate the progress made and the positive impact on overall well-being.

Next Steps:

- Consider if any goals need adjustment or if new goals should be added.
- Continue building on the positive habits established.
- Extend grace and kindness to yourself as you move forward.
- Embrace the journey and the growth that comes with it.

WELCOME TO APRIL

Welcome to April, marking the commencement of the second quarter—a time for renewal, growth, and a focus on mindful living. Our weekly thoughts for this month encapsulate essential principles for a fulfilling and balanced life:

Week One: "Count your blessings, not your problems; gratitude is the antidote to worry." April begins with a reminder to shift our perspective. Let's count our blessings instead of dwelling on problems, recognizing that gratitude serves as a powerful antidote to worry. Cultivating a thankful mindset can transform challenges into opportunities.

Week Two: "Your spiritual journey begins with awareness; it thrives with intention." This week invites us to embark on a spiritual journey grounded in awareness and flourishing through intention. As we deepen our connection with the spiritual aspects of life, let's explore the transformative power of mindfulness and purposeful intention.

Week Three: "Find joy in the ordinary; happiness is hidden in the everyday moments." Amid the hustle and bustle, let's pause to discover joy in the ordinary. Happiness often resides in the simplicity of everyday moments. This week encourages us to savor the beauty of the mundane and find joy in the seemingly routine aspects of life.

WELCOME TO APRIL

Week Four: "Wellness is a journey, not a destination — enjoy the process." As we conclude April, we shift our focus to wellness—a continuous journey rather than a fixed destination. Embrace the process, relishing each step towards holistic well-being. This thought encourages us to enjoy the ongoing journey of self-care and vitality.

Join us in April as we embrace these weekly thoughts, cultivating gratitude, embarking on a spiritual journey, finding joy in the ordinary, and enjoying the transformative process of wellness. Together, let's make this second quarter a period of growth, mindfulness, and positive living.

April

Week 1 "Count your blessings, not your problems; gratitude is the antidote to worry."
This week I will take the following steps on my journey:

GRATITUDE

____

____

____

____

HAPPINESS

____

____

____

____

WELLNESS

____

____

____

____

SPIRITUAL AWARENESS

____

____

____

____

Daily Journal

Daily Journal

Ðaily Journal

Daily Journal

Daily Journal

Ðaily Journal

Daily Journal

April

Week 2 Thought of the week, "Your spiritual journey begins with awareness; it thrives with intention."
This week I will take the following steps on my journey:

GRATITUDE

____

____

____

____

HAPPINESS

____

____

____

____

WELLNESS

____

____

____

____

SPIRITUAL AWARENESS

____

____

____

____

Ðaily Journal

Daily Journal

Ðaily Journal

Ðaily Journal

Daily Journal

Daily Journal

Daily Journal

April

Week 3 "Find joy in the ordinary; happiness is hidden in the everyday moments."
This week I will take the following steps on my journey:

GRATITUDE

____

____

____

____

HAPPINESS

____

____

____

____

WELLNESS

____

____

____

____

SPIRITUAL AWARENESS

____

____

____

____

Ðaily Journal

Daily Journal

Ðaily Journal

Ðaily Journal

Daily Journal

Daily Journal

Ðaily Journal

April

Week 4 "Wellness is a journey, not a destination — enjoy the process."
This week I will take the following steps on my journey:

GRATITUDE

____

____

____

____

HAPPINESS

____

____

____

____

WELLNESS

____

____

____

____

SPIRITUAL AWARENESS

____

____

____

____

Daily Journal

Ðaily Journal

Daily Journal

Daily Journal

Ðaily Journal

Daily Journal

Daily Journal

MONTHLY SPENDING TRACKER

DATE: _______________

DATE	AMOUNT	DESCRIPTION	CASH	CARD
			☐	☐
			☐	☐
			☐	☐
			☐	☐
			☐	☐
			☐	☐
			☐	☐
			☐	☐
			☐	☐
			☐	☐
			☐	☐
			☐	☐
			☐	☐
			☐	☐

NOTES:

____

____

____

WELCOME TO MAY

Welcome to May, a month that beckons us to explore the art of living a harmonious and purposeful life. Our focus for the month revolves around these insightful weekly thoughts:

Week One: "Balance is the key to a healthy life; listen to your body's needs." May begins with a gentle reminder that balance is the cornerstone of a healthy and fulfilling life. Tune in to your body's signals, acknowledging and responding to its needs. May this week be a journey towards equilibrium and well-being.

Week Two: "Create your sunshine; happiness is a state of mind you cultivate." As we step into the second week of May, let's embrace the power of cultivating our sunshine. Happiness is not merely found; it's a state of mind that we create. This thought encourages us to find joy within ourselves and radiate positivity to illuminate our days.

Week Three: "Embrace the sacred dance of self-discovery; spiritual awareness is the rhythm of your soul." In the heart of May, let's embark on a sacred dance of self-discovery. Explore the rhythm of your soul through spiritual awareness. This week invites us to connect with our inner selves, unraveling the layers of our being and embracing the journey of self-awareness.

WELCOME TO MAY

Week Four: "Gratitude is the currency of the heart, spend it generously." As we conclude May, let's appreciate the abundance in our lives. Gratitude is not just felt but actively expressed. Consider it the currency of the heart and spend it generously, fostering connections and enriching the tapestry of our experiences.

Join us in May as we delve into these weekly thoughts, seeking balance, creating our sunshine, embracing self-discovery, and spending the currency of gratitude generously. Together, let's make May a month of growth, joy, and heart-centered living.

 May

Week 1 "Balance is the key to a healthy life; listen to your body's needs."
This week I will take the following steps on my journey:

GRATITUDE

____
____
____
____

HAPPINESS

____
____
____
____

WELLNESS

____
____
____
____

SPIRITUAL AWARENESS

____
____
____
____

Daily Journal

Ðaily Journal

Daily Journal

Daily Journal

Daily Journal

Ðaily Journal

Ðaily Journal

May

Week 2 "Create your sunshine; happiness is a state of mind you cultivate."
This week I will take the following steps on my journey:

GRATITUDE

____

____

____

____

HAPPINESS

____

____

____

____

WELLNESS

____

____

____

____

SPIRITUAL AWARENESS

____

____

____

____

Daily Journal

Daily Journal

Ðaily Journal

Ðaily Journal

Daily Journal

Daily Journal

Daily Journal

May

Week 3 "Embrace the sacred dance of self-discovery; spiritual awareness is the rhythm of your soul."

This week I will take the following steps on my journey:

GRATITUDE

____

____

____

____

HAPPINESS

____

____

____

____

WELLNESS

____

____

____

____

SPIRITUAL AWARENESS

____

____

____

____

Daily Journal

Ðaily Journal

Daily Journal

Đaily Journal

Daily Journal

Ðaily Journal

Ðaily Journal

May

Week 4 "Gratitude is the currency of the heart, spend it generously."
This week I will take the following steps on my journey:

GRATITUDE

____

____

____

____

HAPPINESS

____

____

____

____

WELLNESS

____

____

____

____

SPIRITUAL AWARENESS

____

____

____

____

Daily Journal

Daily Journal

Daily Journal

Ðaily Journal

Ðaily Journal

Daily Journal

Đaily Journal

MONTHLY SPENDING TRACKER

DATE: ___________________

DATE	AMOUNT	DESCRIPTION	CASH	CARD
			☐	☐
			☐	☐
			☐	☐
			☐	☐
			☐	☐
			☐	☐
			☐	☐
			☐	☐
			☐	☐
			☐	☐
			☐	☐
			☐	☐
			☐	☐
			☐	☐

NOTES:

____

____

____

WELCOME TO JUNE

As we bid farewell to the second quarter of the year, June unfolds with a focus on purpose, gratitude, mindful choices, and self-confidence. Our weekly thoughts guide us toward a transformative conclusion to this quarter:

Week One: "In the dance of life, gratitude is the graceful step that leads to happiness." June commences with the metaphorical dance of life, emphasizing gratitude as the graceful step that paves the way to happiness. Let's move through this week with appreciation, recognizing that gratitude can add a rhythm of joy to our existence.

Week Two: "Connect to the divine within; your spirit holds the map to a purposeful existence." In the second week, we delve into the spiritual realm, acknowledging the divine within. Your spirit carries the map to a purposeful existence. By connecting to this inner guidance, we navigate towards a life imbued with meaning and fulfillment.

Week Three: "Happiness is not in the future; it's a choice you make in the present." Mid-June reminds us that happiness is not a distant destination but a choice we make in the present. Let's embrace the power of the now, making conscious choices that contribute to our well-being and bring joy into each moment.

WELCOME TO JUNE

Week Four: "Nourish your body, starve your doubts." As we conclude June, the focus turns to self-confidence and well-being. Nourish your body with care and nutrition, simultaneously starving the doubts that may hinder your path. This week encourages a positive relationship with oneself, fostering both physical and mental resilience.

Join us in this June journey, concluding the second quarter with gratitude, purpose, mindful choices, and self-assurance. Together, let's make these weekly thoughts a guide to a fulfilling and empowered way of life.

June

Week 1 "In the dance of life, gratitude is the graceful step that leads to happiness."
This week I will take the following steps on my journey:

GRATITUDE

____

____

____

____

HAPPINESS

____

____

____

____

WELLNESS

____

____

____

____

SPIRITUAL AWARENESS

____

____

____

____

Daily Journal

Daily Journal

Daily Journal

Daily Journal

Đaily Journal

Daily Journal

Ðaily Journal

June

Week 2 "Connect to the divine within; your spirit holds the map to a purposeful existence."

This week I will take the following steps on my journey:

GRATITUDE

____

____

____

____

HAPPINESS

____

____

____

____

WELLNESS

____

____

____

____

SPIRITUAL AWARENESS

____

____

____

____

Đaily Journal

Daily Journal

Daily Journal

Daily Journal

Ðaily Journal

Daily Journal

Daily Journal

Week 3 "Happiness is not in the future; it's a choice you make in the present."
This week I will take the following steps on my journey:

GRATITUDE

____

____

____

____

HAPPINESS

____

____

____

____

WELLNESS

____

____

____

____

SPIRITUAL AWARENESS

____

____

____

____

Daily Journal

Daily Journal

Daily Journal

Ðaily Journal

Ðaily Journal

Daily Journal

Ðaily Journal

June

Week 4 "Nourish your body, starve your doubts."
This week I will take the following steps on my journey:

GRATITUDE

____
____
____
____

HAPPINESS

____
____
____
____

WELLNESS

____
____
____
____

SPIRITUAL AWARENESS

____
____
____

Daily Journal

Đaily Journal

Daily Journal

Daily Journal

Đaily Journal

Daily Journal

Daily Journal

MONTHLY SPENDING TRACKER

DATE: ______________

DATE	AMOUNT	DESCRIPTION	CASH	CARD
			☐	☐
			☐	☐
			☐	☐
			☐	☐
			☐	☐
			☐	☐
			☐	☐
			☐	☐
			☐	☐
			☐	☐
			☐	☐
			☐	☐
			☐	☐
			☐	☐

NOTES:

____

____

____

Second Quarter Check-In

Congratulations on reaching the midpoint of the year! As we embark on the second quarter check-in, take a moment to acknowledge the incredible progress you've already achieved. Your commitment to personal growth in the realms of Gratitude, Happiness, Spirituality, and Wellness has undoubtedly shaped a significant part of your journey.

This check-in is a celebration of the dedication and effort you've invested in your well-being. It's a chance to appreciate the milestones reached, no matter how small, and to recognize the resilience that has brought you this far.

As we delve into the assessment of your goals, remember that this process is not about perfection but about understanding the evolving nature of your aspirations. Celebrate your successes, embrace the lessons learned from challenges, and extend the same grace to yourself that you would to a dear friend.

This introspective review will guide you in determining whether any goals need refinement or elimination, or if you've successfully achieved them. It's an opportunity to align your objectives with your current values and priorities, ensuring that the path forward is both authentic and fulfilling.

So, let's explore the progress made in Gratitude, Happiness, Spirituality, and Wellness. Your journey is unique, and this check-in is a testament to your commitment to personal well-being. Embrace this moment with positivity and self-compassion, knowing that each step forward is a testament to your growth and resilience.Top of Form

My Goals

GRATITUDE

____

____

____

____

HAPPINESS

____

____

____

____

WELLNESS

____

____

____

____

SPIRITUAL AWARENESS

____

____

____

____

QUARTERLY SPENDING TRACKER

DUE DATE	BILL NAME	AMOUNT	PAID

INCOME	EXPENSES	PROFIT

General Reflection:

- Identify patterns, challenges, or successes across all areas.
- Consider whether any goals need adjustment or elimination.
- Acknowledge the overall progress made since the beginning of the year.

Next Steps:

- Celebrate reaching the halfway point and the growth you've achieved.
- Extend grace to yourself, especially if certain goals need modification.
- Adjust goals as needed to align with your evolving priorities.
- Continue the journey with a sense of positivity and self-compassion.

WELCOME TO JULY

Welcome to July, marking the commencement of the third quarter —a season dedicated to nurturing well-being, finding joy in the present, and fostering gratitude for life's simple pleasures. Our focus for this month is beautifully encapsulated in these insightful weekly thoughts:

Week One: "Every step is a stride towards a healthier you." July begins with a powerful reminder that every step you take is a deliberate stride toward a healthier and more vibrant version of yourself. This week, embrace the journey of well-being, recognizing the transformative impact of small, intentional choices.

Week Two: "Dance to the beat of your happiness; the music is within you." In the second week, let the rhythm of your own happiness guide your steps. Dance to the beat that resonates from within, celebrating the unique melody of your joy. This week encourages self-expression and mindfulness, creating a symphony of positivity.

Week Three: "Sleep is the best meditation for a rejuvenated tomorrow." Mid-July calls for a focus on rejuvenation through restful sleep. Acknowledge that sleep is not just a necessity but a powerful meditation that prepares you for a new day. Prioritize quality sleep to awaken refreshed and ready for life's opportunities.

WELCOME TO JULY

Week Four: "Appreciate the small things; they are the whispers of gratitude." As we conclude July, take a moment to appreciate the small things that often go unnoticed. These subtle moments are the whispers of gratitude, enriching your daily life. Cultivate mindfulness and let gratitude illuminate the beauty found in the simplicity of each day.

Join us in this July journey, where each week invites you to embrace health, dance to your unique happiness, prioritize rejuvenation through sleep, and savor the sweet whispers of gratitude. Together, let's make this month a celebration of well-being and the richness found in life's little joys.

July

Week 1 "Every step is a stride towards a healthier you."

This week I will take the following steps on my journey:

GRATITUDE

____

____

____

____

HAPPINESS

____

____

____

____

WELLNESS

____

____

____

____

SPIRITUAL AWARENESS

____

____

____

____

Daily Journal

Ðaily Journal

Daily Journal

Daily Journal

Daily Journal

Daily Journal

Daily Journal

July

Week 2 "Dance to the beat of your happiness; the music is within you."

This week I will take the following steps on my journey:

GRATITUDE

____

____

____

____

HAPPINESS

____

____

____

____

WELLNESS

____

____

____

____

SPIRITUAL AWARENESS

____

____

____

____

Daily Journal

Ðaily Journal

Daily Journal

Ðaily Journal

Ðaily Journal

Daily Journal

Ðaily Journal

July

Week 3 "Sleep is the best meditation for a rejuvenated tomorrow."
This week I will take the following steps on my journey:

GRATITUDE

____

____

____

____

HAPPINESS

____

____

____

____

WELLNESS

____

____

____

____

SPIRITUAL AWARENESS

____

____

____

____

Daily Journal

Ðaily Journal

Ðaily Journal

Ðaily Journal

Daily Journal

Daily Journal

July

Week 4 "Appreciate the small things; they are the whispers of gratitude."
This week I will take the following steps on my journey:

GRATITUDE

____
____
____
____

HAPPINESS

____
____
____
____

WELLNESS

____
____
____
____

SPIRITUAL AWARENESS

____
____
____
____

Ðaily Journal

Daily Journal

Daily Journal

Ðaily Journal

Daily Journal

Daily Journal

Daily Journal

<h1 style="text-align:center">Monthly Spending Tracker</h1>

DATE: _______________

DATE	AMOUNT	DESCRIPTION	CASH	CARD
			☐	☐
			☐	☐
			☐	☐
			☐	☐
			☐	☐
			☐	☐
			☐	☐
			☐	☐
			☐	☐
			☐	☐
			☐	☐
			☐	☐
			☐	☐
			☐	☐

NOTES:

____

____

____

WELCOME TO AUGUST

Welcome to August, a month where our focus centers on the exploration of gratitude, spiritual awareness, kindness, and mindful investment in our health and wellness. Each week unfolds a distinct theme, guiding us through a journey of self-discovery and purpose:

Week One: "Gratitude is the key that opens the door to abundance." August begins with a profound acknowledgment of gratitude as the key that unlocks the door to abundance. This week invites us to reflect on the richness found in appreciation, fostering a mindset that opens us to the multitude of possibilities that life offers.

Week Two: "Breathe in the essence of your being; spiritual awareness is the art of presence." In the second week, we delve into the art of presence. By breathing in the essence of our being, we nurture spiritual awareness. This week encourages a deep connection with the present moment, allowing us to explore the depth of our inner selves.

Week Three: "Kindness is the language of happiness; speak it fluently." Mid-August calls for the fluent expression of kindness as the language of happiness. This week prompts us to infuse our actions and words with kindness, creating a positive atmosphere that not only uplifts ourselves but also resonates with those around us.

WELCOME TO AUGUST

Week Four: "Your health is an investment, not an expense." As we conclude August, we recognize the importance of viewing health as a valuable investment. This week emphasizes the mindful approach of considering our health as a cornerstone for a vibrant and purposeful life, reinforcing the notion that it is an investment, not a mere expense.

Join us in this August journey, where each week offers a unique exploration of gratitude, presence, kindness, and the conscientious investment in our health. Together, let's make this month a canvas of mindful living and purposeful choices.

Week 1 "Gratitude is the key that opens the door to abundance."
This week I will take the following steps on my journey:

GRATITUDE

____
____
____
____

HAPPINESS

____
____
____
____

WELLNESS

____
____
____
____

SPIRITUAL AWARENESS

____
____
____
____

Ðaily Journal

Daily Journal

Ðaily Journal

Ðaily Journal

Daily Journal

Daily Journal

Ðaily Journal

August

Week 2 "Breathe in the essence of your being; spiritual awareness is the art of presence."

This week I will take the following steps on my journey:

GRATITUDE

____

____

____

____

HAPPINESS

____

____

____

____

WELLNESS

____

____

____

____

SPIRITUAL AWARENESS

____

____

____

____

Đaily Journal

Daily Journal

Ðaily Journal

Daily Journal

Daily Journal

Ðaily Journal

Daily Journal

August

Week 3 "Kindness is the language of happiness; speak it fluently."

This week I will take the following steps on my journey:

GRATITUDE

____

____

____

____

HAPPINESS

____

____

____

____

WELLNESS

____

____

____

____

SPIRITUAL AWARENESS

____

____

____

____

Daily Journal

Ðaily Journal

Daily Journal

Daily Journal

Daily Journal

Daily Journal

Ðaily Journal

August

Week 4 "Your health is an investment, not an expense."

GRATITUDE

____

____

____

____

HAPPINESS

____

____

____

____

WELLNESS

____

____

____

____

SPIRITUAL AWARENESS

____

____

____

____

Daily Journal

Daily Journal

Daily Journal

Đaily Journal

Daily Journal

Daily Journal

Daily Journal

Monthly Spending Tracker

DATE: _______________

DATE	AMOUNT	DESCRIPTION	CASH	CARD
			☐	☐
			☐	☐
			☐	☐
			☐	☐
			☐	☐
			☐	☐
			☐	☐
			☐	☐
			☐	☐
			☐	☐
			☐	☐
			☐	☐
			☐	☐
			☐	☐

NOTES:

____

____

____

WELCOME TO SEPTEMBER

Welcome to September, a month that marks the celebration of the end of the third quarter—a season dedicated to daily practices, meaningful experiences, spiritual awareness, and the harmonious melody of gratitude. Let's embark on this journey with the following weekly thoughts:

Week One: "Well-being is a daily practice, not a sporadic event." September begins with the recognition that well-being is not a sporadic event but a daily practice. This week invites us to embrace the consistent effort required to nurture our overall wellness, creating a foundation for a fulfilling and balanced life.

Week Two: "Chase experiences, not things; true happiness is found in moments, not possessions." In the second week, the focus shifts to the pursuit of experiences over material possessions. True happiness, it suggests, lies in the richness of moments rather than the accumulation of things. Let's actively seek and cherish the experiences that bring joy and fulfillment.

Week Three: "Your spirit is a guiding light; become aware, and let it illuminate your path." Mid-September encourages us to connect with our inner spirit, acknowledging it as a guiding light. By becoming aware of our spiritual essence, we can allow it to illuminate our path, guiding us toward purpose, meaning, and a deeper understanding of ourselves.

WELCOME TO SEPTEMBER

Week Four: "Gratitude is the music of the heart; play it often." As we conclude September, the focus turns to gratitude as the music of the heart. This week prompts us to play the beautiful melody of gratitude often, recognizing its power to enhance our lives and foster a positive and harmonious atmosphere.

Join us in this September celebration, where each week unveils a new facet of daily practices, meaningful experiences, spiritual awareness, and the joyful play of gratitude. Let's make this month a symphony of mindful living and the celebration of a well-lived quarter.

September

Week 1 "Well-being is a daily practice, not a sporadic event."
This week I will take the following steps on my journey:

GRATITUDE

____
____
____
____

HAPPINESS

____
____
____
____

WELLNESS

____
____
____
____

SPIRITUAL AWARENESS

____
____
____
____

Daily Journal

Daily Journal

Ðaily Journal

Daily Journal

Ðaily Journal

Daily Journal

Daily Journal

September

Week 2 "Chase experiences, not things; true happiness is found in moments, not possessions."

This week I will take the following steps on my journey:

GRATITUDE

____

____

____

____

HAPPINESS

____

____

____

____

WELLNESS

____

____

____

____

SPIRITUAL AWARENESS

____

____

____

Daily Journal

Daily Journal

Daily Journal

Ðaily Journal

Ðaily Journal

Daily Journal

Daily Journal

September

Week 3 "Your spirit is a guiding light; become aware, and let it
illuminate your path."
This week I will take the following steps on my journey:

GRATITUDE

____

____

____

____

HAPPINESS

____

____

____

____

WELLNESS

____

____

____

____

SPIRITUAL AWARENESS

____

____

____

____

Ðaily Journal

Daily Journal

Đaily Journal

Daily Journal

Ðaily Journal

Ðaily Journal

Daily Journal

September

Week 4 "Gratitude is the music of the heart; play it often."
This week I will take the following steps on my journey:

GRATITUDE

____

____

____

____

HAPPINESS

____

____

____

____

WELLNESS

____

____

____

____

SPIRITUAL AWARENESS

____

____

____

____

Ðaily Journal

Daily Journal

Daily Journal

Daily Journal

Daily Journal

Daily Journal

Ðaily Journal

Monthly Spending Tracker

DATE: ________________

DATE	AMOUNT	DESCRIPTION	CASH	CARD
			☐	☐
			☐	☐
			☐	☐
			☐	☐
			☐	☐
			☐	☐
			☐	☐
			☐	☐
			☐	☐
			☐	☐
			☐	☐
			☐	☐
			☐	☐
			☐	☐

NOTES:

____

____

____

Third Quarter Check-In

As we stand on the threshold of the final quarter, it's a moment to reflect on the incredible journey of self-discovery and growth you've navigated throughout this year. The challenges faced and the triumphs celebrated have shaped a narrative of resilience and progress. This third quarter check-in is an opportunity to honor the path you've walked, assess the goals set in Gratitude, Happiness, Spirituality, and Wellness, and prepare for a strong and healthy finish to the year.

The journey thus far is a testament to your commitment to well-being, personal development, and a positive mindset. The purpose of this check-in is not only to evaluate your goals but also to acknowledge the strength you've shown in facing both joys and obstacles.

As you delve into this introspection, remember to approach it with kindness and understanding. Reflect on the lessons learned, appreciate the progress made, and use this assessment to fine-tune your goals for the final stretch. Whether you find areas for refinement or celebration, each insight gained will contribute to a more intentional and fulfilling conclusion to the year.

So, let's embark on this third quarter check-in with gratitude for the journey so far, excitement for the growth ahead, and a commitment to finishing the year on a note of health, happiness, and accomplishment.

My Goals

GRATITUDE

____

____

____

____

HAPPINESS

____

____

____

____

WELLNESS

____

____

____

____

SPIRITUAL AWARENESS

____

____

____

____

QUARTERLY PENDING TRACKER

DUE DATE	BILL NAME	AMOUNT	PAID

INCOME	EXPENSES	PROFIT

General Reflection:

- Acknowledge the challenges faced and lessons learned.
- Celebrate the overall growth and resilience demonstrated.
- Recognize the interconnectedness of goals across different domains.

Next Steps:

- Refine goals as needed for the final quarter.
- Embrace the upcoming challenges with confidence.
- Extend grace and kindness to yourself as you approach the finish line.
- Remember, you've got this! The journey is a testament to your strength and commitment.

WELCOME TO OCTOBER

Welcome to October, a month that heralds the commencement of the fourth quarter—a season of gratitude, spiritual awareness, positivity, and the intrinsic connection between inner and outer well-being. Let's embark on this journey with the following weekly thoughts:

Week One: "The more you thank life, the more life gives you to be thankful for." October unfolds with the recognition that gratitude is a powerful force. This week invites us to express our thanks to life, understanding that the more we appreciate, the more life generously offers for us to be thankful for.

Week Two: "In the tapestry of life, spiritual awareness is the thread that weaves purpose and fulfillment." In the second week, we explore the metaphorical tapestry of life. Here, spiritual awareness is the thread that intricately weaves purpose and fulfillment into the fabric of our existence. This thought encourages a deeper connection with our spiritual selves.

Week Three: "Radiate positivity; happiness is contagious." Mid-October calls us to radiate positivity, recognizing that happiness is contagious. Let's become beacons of positivity, spreading joy to those around us and creating a ripple effect of happiness in our communities and beyond.

WELCOME TO OCTOBER

Week Four: "A healthy outside starts from the inside." As we conclude October, the focus turns to the profound connection between inner and outer health. This week emphasizes that a healthy external appearance is a reflection of a nourished internal state. It encourages us to prioritize our inner well-being for a vibrant and healthy outward expression.

Join us in this October celebration, where each week unveils a new aspect of gratitude, spiritual awareness, positivity, and the integral relationship between our inner and outer selves. Let's make this month a canvas of mindful living and purposeful choices as we step into the fourth quarter of the year.

October

Week 1 "The more you thank life, the more life gives you to be thankful for."
This week I will take the following steps on my journey:

GRATITUDE

____

____

____

____

HAPPINESS

____

____

____

____

WELLNESS

____

____

____

____

SPIRITUAL AWARENESS

____

____

____

____

Daily Journal

Daily Journal

Daily Journal

Ðaily Journal

Daily Journal

Ðaily Journal

Daily Journal

October

Week 2 "In the tapestry of life, spiritual awareness is the thread that weaves purpose and fulfillment."
This week I will take the following steps on my journey:

GRATITUDE

____

____

____

____

HAPPINESS

____

____

____

____

WELLNESS

____

____

____

____

SPIRITUAL AWARENESS

____

____

____

____

Ðaily Journal

Daily Journal

Daily Journal

Ðaily Journal

Ðaily Journal

Đaily Journal

Ðaily Journal

October

Week 3 "Radiate positivity; happiness is contagious."
This week I will take the following steps on my journey:

GRATITUDE

____
____
____
____

HAPPINESS

____
____
____
____

WELLNESS

____
____
____
____

SPIRITUAL AWARENESS

____
____
____
____

Daily Journal

Ðaily Journal

Daily Journal

Ðaily Journal

Ðaily Journal

Ðaily Journal

Daily Journal

October

Week 4 "A healthy outside starts from the inside."
This week I will take the following steps on my journey:

GRATITUDE

____

____

____

____

HAPPINESS

____

____

____

____

WELLNESS

____

____

____

____

SPIRITUAL AWARENESS

____

____

____

____

Daily Journal

Đaily Journal

Daily Journal

Daily Journal

Daily Journal

Ðaily Journal

Ðaily Journal

Monthly Spending Tracker

DATE: _______________

DATE	AMOUNT	DESCRIPTION	CASH	CARD
			☐	☐
			☐	☐
			☐	☐
			☐	☐
			☐	☐
			☐	☐
			☐	☐
			☐	☐
			☐	☐
			☐	☐
			☐	☐
			☐	☐
			☐	☐
			☐	☐

NOTES:

____

____

____

WELCOME TO NOVEMBER

Welcome to November, a month that calls us to embrace a focus on health, progress, spiritual awareness, and the transformative power of gratitude. As we embark on this journey, let's delve into the profound insights encapsulated in each weekly thought:

Week One: "Choose health today for a vibrant tomorrow." November commences with an invitation to make mindful choices for our health in the present moment. This week encourages us to prioritize health, recognizing it as a conscious decision that paves the way for a vibrant and flourishing tomorrow.

Week Two: "Celebrate progress, not perfection; happiness is in the journey, not the destination." In the second week, the spotlight is on celebrating progress over the pursuit of perfection. Let's revel in the journey, understanding that true happiness is found in the continuous process of growth, rather than fixating on an idealized destination.

Week Three: "Meditate on your existence; spiritual awareness is the mirror reflecting your divine essence." Mid-November beckons us to turn inward and reflect on our existence. Spiritual awareness becomes the mirror that reveals our divine essence. This week encourages a deeper connection with the profound aspects of our being.

WELCOME TO NOVEMBER

Week Four: "Gratitude is a powerful potion that transforms challenges into opportunities." As November draws to a close, we focus on the transformative power of gratitude. This week emphasizes that gratitude is a potent potion capable of turning challenges into opportunities. Let's cultivate an attitude of thankfulness, finding the positive aspects within every situation.

Join us in this November exploration, where each week unveils a new dimension of health, progress, spiritual awareness, and the alchemical impact of gratitude. Let's make this month a journey of mindful choices and inner reflections, embracing the essence of November's offerings.

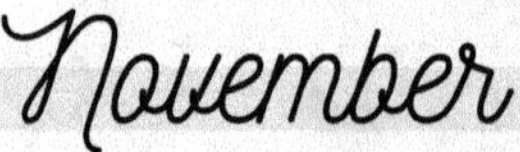

November

Week 1 "Choose health today for a vibrant tomorrow."
This week I will take the following steps on my journey:

GRATITUDE

____

____

____

____

HAPPINESS

____

____

____

____

WELLNESS

____

____

____

____

SPIRITUAL AWARENESS

____

____

____

____

Daily Journal

Ðaily Journal

Ðaily Journal

Ðaily Journal

Ðaily Journal

Ðaily Journal

Daily Journal

Week 2 "Celebrate progress, not perfection; happiness is in the journey, not the destination."
This week I will take the following steps on my journey:

GRATITUDE

____

____

____

____

HAPPINESS

____

____

____

____

WELLNESS

____

____

____

____

SPIRITUAL AWARENESS

____

____

____

____

Daily Journal

Daily Journal

Daily Journal

Ðaily Journal

Daily Journal

Ðaily Journal

Daily Journal

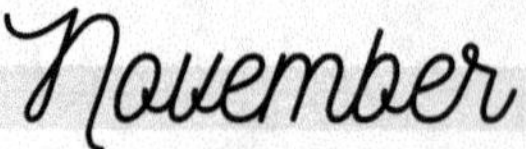 November

Week 3 "Meditate on your existence; spiritual awareness is the mirror reflecting your divine essence."

This week I will take the following steps on my journey:

GRATITUDE

____

____

____

____

HAPPINESS

____

____

____

____

WELLNESS

____

____

____

____

SPIRITUAL AWARENESS

____

____

____

____

Ðaily Journal

Daily Journal

Ðaily Journal

Ðaily Journal

Ðaily Journal

Daily Journal

Daily Journal

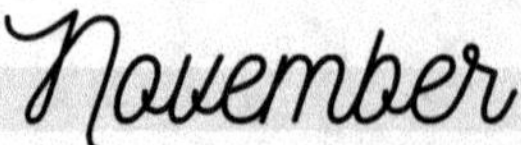

November

Week 4 "Gratitude is a powerful potion that transforms challenges into opportunities."

This week I will take the following steps on my journey:

GRATITUDE

____

____

____

____

HAPPINESS

____

____

____

____

WELLNESS

____

____

____

____

SPIRITUAL AWARENESS

____

____

____

____

Ðaily Journal

Daily Journal

Daily Journal

Ðaily Journal

Ðaily Journal

Daily Journal

Ðaily Journal

Monthly Spending Tracker

DATE: _______________

DATE	AMOUNT	DESCRIPTION	CASH	CARD
			☐	☐
			☐	☐
			☐	☐
			☐	☐
			☐	☐
			☐	☐
			☐	☐
			☐	☐
			☐	☐
			☐	☐
			☐	☐
			☐	☐
			☐	☐
			☐	☐

NOTES:

____

____

____

WELCOME TO DECEMBER

Welcome to December, a month that not only marks the year-end but also signifies the conclusion of the fourth quarter—a time for reflection, spiritual exploration, acceptance, and mindful communication between mind and body. As we embrace the essence of these weekly thoughts, let's delve into the profound insights they offer:

Week One: "Start and end your day with gratitude; it's the secret sauce for a fulfilling life." December commences with a reminder that gratitude enriches the flavor of a fulfilling life. This week encourages us to infuse our mornings and evenings with the essence of thankfulness, creating a harmonious rhythm for our days.

Week Two: "Tune into your soul's frequency; spiritual awareness is the melody of self-discovery." In the second week, we embark on a journey of self-discovery through spiritual awareness. Our souls carry a unique frequency, and this week invites us to tune into that inner melody, guiding us in understanding ourselves more deeply.

Week Three: "Let go of what you can't control; happiness blooms in acceptance." Mid-December urges us to release the grasp on the uncontrollable aspects of life. Happiness, It suggests, flourishes in the fertile ground of acceptance. This week encourages us to let go of unnecessary burdens and find contentment in embracing the ebb and flow of life.

WELCOME TO DECEMBER

Week Four: "Your body hears everything your mind says; speak health." As we conclude December and bid farewell to the year, the focus turns to the profound connection between mind and body. This week emphasizes the impact of our thoughts on our physical well-being. Let's speak health to our minds, fostering positive communication that resonates throughout our entire being.

Take time to acknowledge accomplishments and celebrate you! In the spirit of the year-end, reflect on your achievements, both big and small. Celebrate the journey you've traveled and the growth you've experienced. As December unfolds, let these weekly thoughts guide you in embracing the essence of self-appreciation and reflection.

December

Week 1 "Start and end your day with gratitude; it's the secret sauce for a fulfilling life."

This week I will take the following steps on my journey:

GRATITUDE

____

____

____

____

HAPPINESS

____

____

____

____

WELLNESS

____

____

____

____

SPIRITUAL AWARENESS

____

____

____

____

Daily Journal

Daily Journal

Ðaily Journal

Ðaily Journal

Daily Journal

Daily Journal

Daily Journal

December

Week 2 "Tune into your soul's frequency; spiritual awareness is the melody of self-discovery."

This week I will take the following steps on my journey:

GRATITUDE

____

____

____

____

HAPPINESS

____

____

____

____

WELLNESS

____

____

____

____

SPIRITUAL AWARENESS

____

____

____

____

Daily Journal

Ðaily Journal

Daily Journal

Daily Journal

Daily Journal

Daily Journal

Daily Journal

December

Week 3 "Let go of what you can't control; happiness blooms in acceptance."
This week I will take the following steps on my journey:

GRATITUDE

____
____
____
____

HAPPINESS

____
____
____
____

WELLNESS

____
____
____
____

SPIRITUAL AWARENESS

____
____
____

Ðaily Journal

Daily Journal

Đaily Journal

Ðaily Journal

Ðaily Journal

Ðaily Journal

Daily Journal

December

Week 4 "Your body hears everything your mind says; speak health."
This week I will take the following steps on my journey:

GRATITUDE

____

____

____

____

HAPPINESS

____

____

____

____

WELLNESS

____

____

____

____

SPIRITUAL AWARENESS

____

____

____

____

Ðaily Journal

Daily Journal

Đaily Journal

Daily Journal

Daily Journal

Ðaily Journal

Daily Journal

MONTHLY SPENDING TRACKER

DATE: _______________

DATE	AMOUNT	DESCRIPTION	CASH	CARD
			☐	☐
			☐	☐
			☐	☐
			☐	☐
			☐	☐
			☐	☐
			☐	☐
			☐	☐
			☐	☐
			☐	☐
			☐	☐
			☐	☐
			☐	☐
			☐	☐

NOTES:

____

____

____

Fourth Quarter Check-In

Congratulations on reaching the finish line of this transformative year! As we approach the conclusion of this chapter, it's time to reflect on the incredible journey you've undertaken toward becoming your healthiest self. While not every goal may have been achieved, the progress made is a testament to your resilience, dedication, and growth.

This fourth quarter check-in serves as a moment of acknowledgment and celebration. It's an opportunity to recognize the three individuals who will never be in the same room together— the person you were, the person you are, and the person you are becoming. Your journey is a continuous evolution, and each step has brought you closer to your authentic self.

As you assess the progress made in Gratitude, Happiness, Spirituality, and Wellness, remember that this is not just an end but a transition into a new beginning. Take a deep breath, appreciate the lessons learned, and regroup for the start of the next year's journey.

My Goals

GRATITUDE

____

____

____

____

HAPPINESS

____

____

____

____

WELLNESS

____

____

____

____

SPIRITUAL AWARENESS

____

____

____

____

QUARTERLY SPENDING TRACKER

DUE DATE	BILL NAME	AMOUNT	PAID

INCOME	EXPENSES	PROFIT

General Reflection:

- Embrace the journey and growth experienced throughout the year.
- Recognize the resilience demonstrated in overcoming challenges.
- Understand that the journey toward your healthiest self is ongoing.

Next Steps:

- Breathe and savor the achievements, no matter how small.
- Regroup and prepare for the start of the next year's journey.
- Set new intentions, goals, and aspirations for the coming year.
- Remember, you are well on your way to becoming the person you aspire to be. Embrace the journey ahead with open arms.

ANNUAL FINANCES

Financial Goals

1.
2.
3.
4.
5.
6.

Action Steps

1.
2.
3.
4.
5.
6.

January

	Target	Actual
Income		
Expenses		

February

	Target	Actual
Income		
Expenses		

March

	Target	Actual
Income		
Expenses		

April

	Target	Actual
Income		
Expenses		

May

	Target	Actual
Income		
Expenses		

June

	Target	Actual
Income		
Expenses		

July

	Target	Actual
Income		
Expenses		

August

	Target	Actual
Income		
Expenses		

September

	Target	Actual
Income		
Expenses		

October

	Target	Actual
Income		
Expenses		

November

	Target	Actual
Income		
Expenses		

December

	Target	Actual
Income		
Expenses		

Whole Year Overview

Target Income		Difference		Actual Income		Difference
Target Expenses				Actual Expenses		

End of the Year Reflection

Welcome to this moment of reflection and celebration as we mark the completion of another year on our journey toward personal growth and fulfillment. In this section, we invite you to embark on a heartfelt retrospective, where we celebrate our achievements, acknowledge setbacks, and prepare ourselves for the adventures that lie ahead.

Over the past year, we've dedicated ourselves to cultivating gratitude, nurturing happiness, prioritizing wellness, and deepening our spiritual connection. As we flip through the pages of our journal, we are reminded of the milestones we've reached, the challenges we've overcome, and the moments of pure joy that have enriched our lives.

In this space of introspection, we honor ourselves for the dedication and perseverance we've demonstrated in pursuit of our goals. We celebrate the victories, both big and small, recognizing the progress we've made and the growth we've experienced along the way.

However, amidst the celebrations, we also acknowledge the setbacks and obstacles that may have crossed our path. These moments serve as valuable lessons, teaching us resilience, humility, and the importance of embracing imperfection.

As we prepare to turn the page and welcome a new year, let us do so with optimism and intention. Take this opportunity to set new goals, envision the life you wish to create, and commit to nurturing your well-being with love and compassion.

And now, we invite you to write a letter to your future self—a message of hope and encouragement that will serve as a guiding light on your journey forward. Feel free to pour your heart onto the next few pages, infuse it with love, and trust that the words you write today will inspire and uplift you in the days to come.

Meditative Moments

"Meditative Moments," are 5-minute meditations crafted to bookend your day with serenity and mindfulness. In the hustle and bustle of our daily lives, finding extended periods for meditation can be challenging, but everyone can spare a precious 5 minutes. In this section, we invite you to pause, breathe, and center yourself in moments of quiet reflection.

These simple meditations focus on the areas of Gratitude, Spiritual Awareness, Happiness, and Wellness. I encourage you to utilize these mediations throughout your day and on your journey to help you remain centered and focused.

Gratitude Meditation: Begin your day with a heart full of gratitude. Take these 5 minutes to reflect on the positive aspects of your life. Cultivating gratitude can set a positive tone for the day ahead, fostering an appreciation for the beauty that surrounds you.

Spiritual Awareness Meditation: In the middle of your day, reconnect with your spiritual self. Whether you follow a specific religious path or simply seek a deeper connection with the universe, these 5 minutes are an opportunity to tap into your spiritual awareness and find a sense of purpose and meaning.

Happiness Meditation: As the day unfolds, take a short break to focus on happiness. Engage in thoughts and feelings that bring joy and contentment. This meditation is designed to uplift your spirits, allowing you to navigate challenges with a positive mindset and a resilient heart.

Wellness Meditation: Towards the end of your day, prioritize your well-being. Use these 5 minutes to check in with your body and mind. Releasing tension, promoting relaxation, and fostering self-care, this meditation aims to leave you feeling rejuvenated and ready for a restful night's sleep.

Awareness Meditation: Close your day with a moment of heightened awareness. Reflect on the events of the day, acknowledge your emotions, and find a sense of closure. This meditation helps you transition into a state of tranquility, preparing you for a peaceful night's rest.

Remember, in the ebb and flow of life, it's not about finding time; it's about making time. Join us in these Meditative Moments, where just 5 minutes can make a world of difference in your overall well-being. Embrace the power of brief yet impactful mindfulness, allowing yourself the gift of presence amid life's constant motion.

<u>Gratitude Mediation</u>

Welcome to this five-minute meditation focused on self-gratitude, appreciating your accomplishments, and listening to your inner voice for guidance. Find a quiet and comfortable space where you can sit or lie down. Close your eyes and take a few deep breaths to center yourself. Let's begin.

[1 minute] Start by bringing your attention to your breath. Inhale deeply, filling your lungs with fresh air, and exhale slowly, releasing any tension. Feel the rise and fall of your chest and abdomen with each breath. As you breathe, allow yourself to let go of any stress or worries.

[1 minute] Now, shift your focus to gratitude. Bring to mind three things you are grateful for about yourself. They could be qualities, accomplishments, or experiences that make you proud. With each breath, acknowledge and appreciate these aspects of yourself. Feel a sense of warmth and gratitude for who you are.

[1 minute] As you continue to breathe, visualize a golden light surrounding you. This light represents the positive energy of your accomplishments and the gratitude you have for yourself. With each inhale, imagine this light growing brighter and expanding, filling your entire being with warmth and positivity.

[1 minute] Shift your attention to your inner voice. Allow any thoughts or feelings to arise without judgment. Listen to the wisdom within you. What guidance or insights does your inner voice offer? Trust that you have the answers within. As you breathe, create space for your inner voice to be heard.

[1 minute] Now, gently bring your awareness back to the present moment. Wiggle your fingers and toes, and when you're ready, open your eyes. Take a moment to reflect on the gratitude you cultivated and the guidance from your inner voice. Carry this sense of self-appreciation with you as you go about your day.

Remember that self-gratitude is a practice, and by regularly taking the time to appreciate yourself, you can cultivate a positive and compassionate relationship with the most important person in your life—YOU.

Spiritual Awareness Meditation

Welcome to this five-minute meditation focused on healing, spiritual wellness, and connecting with your inner spirit. Find a quiet and comfortable space where you can sit or lie down. Close your eyes and take a few deep breaths to center yourself. Let's begin.

[1 minute] Begin by turning your attention inward. Take a deep breath in, and as you exhale, release any tension you may be holding in your body. With each breath, let go of the outside world and turn your focus inward.

[1 minute] Visualize a healing light surrounding you. This light is pure and radiant, filled with love and positive energy. With each breath, imagine this light entering your body, flowing through every cell, bringing healing and restoration to any areas that need it.

[1 minute] Bring your awareness to your spiritual connection. Imagine a golden thread extending from your heart center, connecting you to a higher source of wisdom and love. Feel the strength of this connection, knowing that you are supported and guided by a higher power.

[1 minute] As you continue to breathe, invite your spirit to speak to you. Ask for guidance on making healthy decisions and maintaining spiritual wellness. Trust that the answers will come in the form of intuition, feelings, or insights. Be open to receiving the wisdom that your spirit has to offer.

[1 minute] Now, take a moment to express gratitude for the spiritual connection you've experienced. Feel a sense of deep appreciation for the healing energy and guidance that surrounds you. With each breath, let this gratitude fill your heart.

When you're ready, gently bring your awareness back to the present moment. Wiggle your fingers and toes and open your eyes. Carry this sense of spiritual wellness and connection with you as you navigate your day.

Happiness Mediation

Welcome to this five-minute meditation focused on cultivating happiness, acknowledging challenges, and fostering positive connections in your life. Find a comfortable position, close your eyes, and let's begin.

[**1 minute**] Start by taking a few deep breaths, allowing your body to relax with each exhale. Acknowledge any tension or thoughts that may be present. With each breath, create space for peace and stillness within.

[1 minute] Now, reflect on the challenges or difficult moments you've faced. Acknowledge them without judgment. Consider the lessons they've brought and the strength they've cultivated within you. Breathe in acceptance, and as you exhale, release any lingering negative energy.

[1 minute] Shift your focus to the positive aspects of your life. Bring to mind moments of joy, accomplishment, or gratitude. Feel the warmth of these positive experiences, allowing them to fill your heart with happiness.

[1 minute] Consider the joy that comes from making others happy. Visualize a circle of light expanding from your heart, reaching out to those around you. Think of ways you can bring happiness to others, whether through a kind word, a gesture, or simply by being present. Feel the interconnectedness of joy.

[1 minute] Express gratitude for the people in your life who bring positivity and joy. Think of someone specific and mentally send them a compliment or a thank you. Acknowledge the role they play in making your life more enjoyable.

As you continue with your day, consider the following questions:
• What changes can you make in your life to increase happiness and meaning?
• Are there aspects of your work or daily routine that could be adjusted to align better with your passions and strengths?
• Do you generally focus on the positive aspects of situations, even when faced with challenges?

When you're ready, gently bring your awareness back to the present moment. Wiggle your fingers and toes and open your eyes. Carry the positivity and happiness you've cultivated into the rest of your day.

<u>Wellness Mediation</u>

Welcome to this five-minute meditation focused on overall wellness, encompassing both physical and financial well-being. Find a quiet and comfortable space, and let's begin.

[1 minute] Start by taking a deep breath in, filling your lungs with fresh air. As you exhale, release any tension in your body. Let each breath be a reminder of the life-sustaining energy flowing through you.

[1 minute] Shift your attention to your heartbeat. Place your hand on your chest and feel the steady rhythm. Recognize the strength and vitality within your body, appreciating the work of your heart.

[1 minute] Now, bring awareness to your body's temperature. Notice the warmth or coolness you feel. Allow a sense of comfort to envelop you, embracing the balance within.

[1 minute] Focus on your temperament. Acknowledge any emotions or sensations without judgment. Let them flow through you, creating space for calm and balance within your emotional state.

[1 minute] Expand your awareness to the air and sounds around you. Feel the gentle flow of the air against your skin and listen to the ambient sounds in your environment. Let these sensations bring a sense of peace and tranquility.

[1 minute] As you continue to breathe, extend your focus to financial wellness. Visualize a stream of clear and positive energy flowing into your financial decisions. Imagine making choices that align with both your short-term and long-term financial well-being.

[1 minute] Call on calming, healthy, and healing energy to surround you. Envision a protective and supportive light enveloping your entire being, physically and financially.

As you conclude this meditation, carry a sense of balance, calm, and positive energy with you. Remember that wellness is a holistic concept, encompassing both the physical and financial aspects of your life.

When you're ready, gently bring your awareness back to the present moment. Wiggle your fingers and toes and open your eyes. Carry this sense of overall wellness into the rest of your day.

Sexual Wellness Meditation

Welcome to this five-minute meditation focused on sexual wellness. Find a comfortable and private space, and let's embark on this journey of self-discovery and healthy connection.

[1 minute] Begin by taking a deep breath in, allowing yourself to fully relax. As you exhale, release any tension in your body. Acknowledge that your body is your own, deserving of pleasure and fulfillment.

[1 minute] Shift your focus to your breath, allowing it to become slow and intentional. With each inhale, visualize positive and empowering energy entering your body. As you exhale, release any negative thoughts or judgments you may hold about your sexuality.

[1 minute] Bring awareness to your body and its sensations. Honor and appreciate its unique responses. Recognize that your desires are natural and valid. You deserve to experience pleasure and to communicate your desires openly and confidently.

[1 minute] Visualize a warm, gentle light surrounding you, representing the liberating energy of self-acceptance. Embrace the freedom to express your needs and wants in a healthy and consensual way. Picture any unhealthy sexual behaviors or habits dissipating, leaving space for positive and fulfilling experiences.

[1 minute] Extend your thoughts to your partner or future partner. Envision open communication, understanding, and shared pleasure. See the connection between the two of you as a dance of mutual satisfaction and joy.

As you conclude this meditation, carry with you a sense of empowerment and self-love. Remember that sexual wellness is an integral part of overall well-being, deserving of attention and care.

When you're ready, gently bring your awareness back to the present moment. Wiggle your fingers and toes and open your eyes. Carry this positive and empowering energy into your sexual experiences and relationships.

Healthy Relationships Meditation

Welcome to this five-minute meditation centered on building and maintaining healthy relationships with a focus on healthy communication, understanding, acceptance, and openness. Find a comfortable and quiet space, and let's begin.

[1 minute] Start by taking a deep breath in, filling your lungs with air, and exhaling any tension. As you breathe, let go of any stress or expectations. Allow yourself to be present in this moment.

[1 minute] Shift your focus to the concept of healthy communication. Picture a bridge forming between you and others, built on openness and honesty. Envision words flowing with kindness and clarity, creating a foundation for understanding.

[1 minute] Bring your attention to the idea of understanding. Imagine a space where empathy and compassion thrive. See yourself and those around you truly comprehending each other's perspectives without judgment.

[1 minute] Reflect on acceptance. Envision a warm and inviting atmosphere where differences are embraced. Picture a garden of diverse flowers, each contributing to the beauty of the whole.

[1 minute] Focus on setting and maintaining healthy boundaries. Imagine a circle of protection around you, allowing you to express your needs and limits with confidence. Envision these boundaries fostering respect and enhancing the quality of your relationships.

When you're ready, gently bring your awareness back to the present moment. Wiggle your fingers and toes and open your eyes. Carry this sense of connection and balance into your interactions and relationships.

Anxiety and Restful Sleep Meditation

Welcome to this five-minute meditation designed to promote a good night's sleep, ease anxiety, and curb restlessness. Find a comfortable and quiet space, and let's begin.

[1 minute] Start by finding a comfortable position, either sitting or lying down. Close your eyes and take a few deep breaths. Inhale calmness, and exhale tension. Let each breath ground you in the present moment.

[1 minute] Shift your focus to your body. Starting from your toes, imagine a gentle wave of relaxation washing over you with each breath. Allow this wave to travel slowly up through your body, releasing any tension it encounters.

[1 minute] Bring your attention to your breath. Inhale deeply, counting to four, and exhale slowly, counting to six. Focus on the rhythm of your breath, letting it become steady and soothing.

[1 minute] Address any anxiety or restlessness. Visualize a box in your mind. As you inhale, trace the top of the box in your mind, counting to four. Pause for a count of four. Exhale as you trace the side of the box, counting to six. Pause again for a count of four. Repeat this box-breathing technique, allowing your mind to focus and your body to relax.

[1 minute] Shift your awareness to a calming scene. Imagine yourself in a peaceful place, whether it's a beach, a forest, or a serene meadow. Engage your senses by picturing the sights, sounds, and sensations of this tranquil environment.

As you conclude this meditation, carry with you a sense of calmness and relaxation. Allow these feelings to guide you into a restful night's sleep.

When you're ready, gently bring your awareness back to the present moment. Wiggle your fingers and toes and open your eyes. Carry this tranquility with you as you transition into sleep.

About the Author

M. Nickleson Battle, Jr., Ed.D., known professionally as "Dr. Nick," is a highly accomplished and compassionate mental health professional, educator, and community leader with licensure as a counselor and clinical supervisor in Virginia, Maryland, and the District of Columbia. Dr. Nick's commitment to addressing complex and sensitive issues is evident through his certifications as a trauma specialist and Telehealth professional, accredited by the National Board of Certified Counselors, showcasing his dedication to delivering accessible and impactful mental health care.

Boasting an impressive academic background, Dr. Nick holds a Doctorate in Education in Counseling Psychology from Argosy University, a Bachelor of Science in Psychology, and a Master of Science Degree in Psychology with a specialization in Leadership Coaching and Development from Capella University. These credentials underline his deep knowledge and unwavering commitment to the field of counseling.

Dr. Nick's clinical specialties include men's mental health, BIPOC trauma, and LGBTQ+ issues, reflecting his dedication to addressing the unique and diverse needs of his clients. His contributions extend beyond the counseling room, as he is the co-host of the "Liberated Minds: Decolonizing Faith, Healing, Mental Health, Sex, and Black Culture" podcast. He has authored articles and delivered extensive presentations on critical topics, enriching the field's understanding.

In his role as an adjunct faculty member, Dr. Nick shares his expertise with the next generation of mental health professionals, holding positions in the Psychology Department at Stevenson University and the Counselor Education program at Johns Hopkins University

You can contact and follow me on social media:

Instagram: drmnicklesonbattlejr
Facebook: Drmnicklesonbattlejr
Website: drmnicklesonbattlejr.com

www.ingramcontent.com/pod-product-compliance
Lightning Source LLC
Chambersburg PA
CBHW050312160726
48002CB00001B/4